NOT WITH YOUR LEGS CROSSED

#SPIRITUALBIRTHINGUNCENSORED

ISBN: 978-1-7350143-9-5

LOC ID: 2021941766

Publisher, Editor and Book Design: Fiery Beacon Publishing House, LLC

Fiery Beacon Consulting and Publishing Group

This work was produced in Greensboro, North Carolina, United States of America.

NOT WITH YOUR LEGS

CROSSED!

#SPRITUALBIRTHINGUNCENSORED

Brandi L. Rojas

TABLE OF CONTENTS

THE DEDICATION:

To my children, Malachi and Sarai, I am honored to be your mother. It is a badge of honor to be entrusted to birth a Prophet and one who God always hears and responds to.

To every visionary that has ever had to birth forth anything bigger than yourself, may the manifestation of what you have been carrying reach to the far places of the Earth. #GoForth

In memory of an amazing leader, mentor and the one God used to affirm me as a Midwife in the spirit,

Apostle Regina McNeill. I will forever love and miss her!

In memory of Mama Lonnette Johnson, a dedicated intercessor, lover and pusher of all, and one that with the flash of her smile and calm in her voice always had a way of letting you know that everything will be just fine.

THE INTRODUCTION

Hello to you, you and you all the way in the back of the room. I pray that this book finds you well and in good spirit. As I type this introduction, I find myself in an extreme place of gratitude and thankfulness that God would allow me the extra time needed for this project to come forth. I found myself in 2019 holding this baby in the depth of my womb, asking God for strength to push. The moment He gave it to me it was immediately dispensed to the next person or emergency that seemed to require more attention than the pain of my contractions and the reality of my labor. Can you relate? Maybe, right now as you are reading this book you are thinking about how much you have endured for the sake of the dream that resides on the inside of you. Possibly in this moment you are even considering what you have put off for the sake of others' emergencies. Let me make this very clear, this book is not about overcoming them or even helping them to push. This book is for YOU – the one who has put off your push.

During the course of our time together, my prayer is that you will find within these pages, words to ignite you and forcefully and lovingly "push" you in pursuit mode. My prayer is that the voice of every contending force will become silent and that you, yes you, will refuse to hold back the greatness that resides in you. My prayer is that you will want your future more than you want your fear and that you will not stop until you accomplish purpose. So, let's get it, let's go!

MIDWIVES ON STRIKE

If there is one lesson I can say that I have learned that shocked me, it was the truth of being a midwife and wanting to go on strike! When we look up the definition of "strike" we find these words:

[1]**"hit forcibly and deliberately with one's hand or a weapon or other implement; a refusal to work organized by a body of employees as a form of protest, typically in an attempt to gain a concession or concessions from their employer."**

At first glance, you would think that the focus would be on the second definition, but if I can be honest, I believe we need to focus on this as a blend of the two. You see, though you may think of a natural midwife going on strike, there are probably just as many SPIRITUAL midwives that desire to go on strike as well. Just a few short weeks ago, I came to the realization of the responsibility of the spiritual midwife in the life of a believer. Midwives, if we are not careful, we can find ourselves in a place of being so involved that we overstep our role. Let me give you an example; Exodus 1:19 says this,

[19] **The midwives answered Pharaoh, "Because the Hebrew women are not like the Egyptian women; they are vigorous and give birth quickly and their babies are born before the midwife can get to them."**

Exodus 1:19 (AMP)

There are midwives in this world who have taken on the role of attempting to convince people that they want to produce, get pregnant and birth out promise! Note the above scripture – the

---

[1] www.google.com

midwife did not show up PRIOR to the conception of the baby but instead at the time of birth. You do not find one word where either midwife says, "Hey! You don't have to do this – let me switch places with you. I'll be your 'on the spot' surrogate!" Instead, we find out that the ones the midwives came to assist were so ready to birth their promise that by the time the midwives arrived the blessing had already shown up.

Let me be clear Midwife, it is your role to help prepare, train and assist the vessel in the process of birthing, but it is NOT your job to make them want the blessing or even to convince them to push- there has to be an inner desire inside of them to make that happen. It is your responsibility to coach and encourage but it is NOT your responsibility to switch places with them and birth out the baby on their behalf – that is NOT your JOB! I believe that there are many midwives who have grown tired simply because they have found themselves surrounded by those who do not even have the will to push but are willing to hold the promise as long as they do not have to be the one who labors for it.

So, Midwife, stop, breathe. The same thing you tell them is the same thing I need you to do in this moment. Stop. Breathe. Know that if they do not want the pregnancy or the process, that is not on you, but simply their decision. Stop Midwife. Breathe. Wipe your sweat, blood and tears. Release those moments where you have cried for others who have decided not to see the greatness that sits before them. Stop. Breathe. Open your eyes and receive those who are ready for the push. Stop. Breathe. KNOW that God did not make a mistake when He chose you – and this mantle called MIDWIFE will not be wasted.

CONTRACTION 1:

It May be Bigger, But You Won't Die

Oftentimes, we are plagued with the qualifying factors of a person and begin to wonder how a person even received the authority to speak on certain subjects. For some you may be wondering if I am a life coach or if I possess a master's degree of some sort. Truthfully, the answer is NO to both, however through so many opportunities, growing pains, lessons learned, losses and wins, I am still here to tell the story. As I begin, I feel that it is only right to give you a background of who I am and a glimpse of what I have endured in this area.

I am a visionary. It took me years to admit that. I am the product of a broken home, the baby of the family and yes, the "black sheep" too. I have accomplished much but still have so far to go. To my knowledge, I am one of the first in my family line to pursue full-time entrepreneurship and even today, am the only female ordained Elder in my father's family line (and possibly my mother's as well.) I am a Pastor and have served in ministry for over ten years; for over eight of those years, I have had the honor of serving with my amazing husband and Senior Pastor of this great vision called Maximizing Life Family Worship Center. When I look at my life now, you could not have convinced me that this would have been me twelve or more years ago. I was broken, ashamed, conflicted and almost consumed with depression. Back then you could not have convinced me that I would ever be a Pastor, mentor, visionary or anything close to it. Quite honestly, you could have never convinced me that I was ever worthy of birthing something bigger than me.

March 15, 2013, proved a collective of people wrong, including myself. The day that I found out that I was "officially"

11

pregnant, my son went with me and sat in the waiting room with me. I knew it in my gut, no pun intended, that I was pregnant, but I needed that last documented confirmation. As we sat, I watched the nurse that took my blood. She scurried around and before I knew it was walking up the hall with a bag and a huge smile on her face. "Congratulations, Mrs. Rojas, you're pregnant!" I smiled; Malachi cheered but I promise you in that moment time completely stood still. After thanking her all I could say was, "Ok, here we go!" My husband of course already knew, so me texting him to give him the news was no surprise. Truth is, we had spoken about children before we got married and had even chosen names but had never considered how fast it would all transpire. I mean like literally - while many come back from their honeymoon with t-shirts and key chains, we came home with a baby! Have you ever found yourself in this place? You speak the desire or the dream and then BOOM, it becomes your reality. Moments like this leave us almost asking God to slow down until we realize how long we have waited.

As the days and weeks progressed, I knew immediately that this pregnancy was different. I found myself with a whole different set of symptoms as compared to my son which seemed to have barely any at all. I went from constant morning sickness to a craving for shelled sunflower seeds and a red solo cup to spit in. (Remember, this is uncensored!) I went from eating whatever I wanted to just eating Triscuits, which was the only thing I could really hold down. As the pregnancy continued, it seemed as if my baby grew overnight and before we knew it the time had come for us to find out the sex of our baby. There we were waiting for the confirmation and wondering which name would be the winner (yes, we had already picked names out, too.) The tech looked and said, "Do you see that right there? It's a GIRL!" My husband and I were excited but if I can be honest, we did not cry and lose it in their office because we knew it was a girl; we just felt it. Now my son on the other hand was

12

betting for a boy, but once he realized that he would be the big brother and protector to his little sister, he was just as excited.

During the months preparing for baby girl's arrival, so much changed and transpired, apart from my body as a whole. From launching into ministry full time, being installed as Pastors, adjusting to married life and the list goes on, it seemed as if the shifting would not end anytime soon. Towards the latter part of my pregnancy, I began getting the big question:

"Are you sure that you are having one baby? Are you sure you don't have one hiding behind the other?"

Every time they asked me, my husband and I both immediately replied, "No! There is only one!" From the moment we found out we were having a girl, we immediately called her by name, Sarai which means "Princess" and from the womb and until this very day, she remains to be just that, a princess. One day someone took the "twin" version to another level:

Them: No twins?

Me: Absolutely not!

Them: Hmm, okay. So, what if you aren't having twins but your baby is, say ten or more pounds.

Me: God would not do that to me – He knows I don't deliver anything over seven pounds.

How cocky! I look back on myself now realizing that in that moment I subconsciously rejected expansion, but we will get to that later. By March 1, 2013, I was done, and I mean done. While people were talking about how much I was glowing, I was trying to overcome my little girl's heel pressing in on my lungs. I found myself telling my doctor that they needed to "get her out," (yes, I used those words) but she simply advised me that we would not induce me until

13

they watched me for another week. When the next appointment came, I walked in with a face that said, "I told you so," to which my doctor replied, "Fix ya' face and let's get you scheduled to have this baby!"

So, the day finally came, and I was ready. I was ready to meet my baby but also ready to get my body back! I walked the hospital with my head up and gleaming with excitement, knowing that by the time that day was over I was going to meet what I had carried for so long. After being processed, I changed, and they got the IV started; I did not like that part at all but was willing to bear it if it would bring me closer to the manifestation of seeing my baby's darling face. That day my family told my son that by the time the day was over, he would be a big brother and I echoed the same sentiments. My midwife came to check on me, and after her review made the determination that additional measures would need to be taken to ensure the safe birth of our daughter. I did not understand then but over time it made sense why they took the precautions that they did. Now, being that I had been through labor and delivery before in my mind I knew exactly how this was going to go – I was going to walk in, push, push, push, chill at the hospital and go home, but my plan that day was not God's plan.

My doctor finally came in. After greeting my husband, mother and I, she advised me that a monitor would need to be put on my baby just to ensure her heartbeat and everything was good. I did not ask any questions since I had monitors with my son as well. This time the difference was that the monitors would have to physically be inserted to be effective. At that moment, my only concern was getting an ETA on my epidural, as I had already told them upon scheduling that not having one was not an option. Having the monitors put in was one of the worst pains I have ever experienced. I was not even in labor at that point but the pressure and pain of it all had my cringing in my bed and caused tears to well up in my eyes. Despite the pain of it all, I made it. My anesthesiologist finally

14

showed up with epidural in hand. After giving me all the side effects, I replied, "Yea! We're good! I've been through this before, let's go!" They completed the procedure, but I still felt pain on one side. After letting the staff know, they determined that my body would have to be turned to the OTHER side for the medicine to take effect. I had never heard of this method, but again, I was just ready to see my blessing! In that moment I did not care about the side effects or thin possibility of paralysis, I just wanted to be able to deliver painlessly; this alone is a word for someone, maybe even you.

The process of labor lasted all day and before I knew it, day had turned to dusk and night. Finally, upon what felt like check number 5,000, I was advised that it was time to push, and boy was I ready! I had already experienced so much in this day, so it could not be any more than that right? My feet went up in the stirrups like a champ, as I reflected about when I had my son and despite all of the differences, I assumed that I had the process down. My doctor said, "PUSH," so I pushed. She asked again, and I obliged again. I cannot tell you what push it was that let her know that something was wrong. I remember wondering and maybe even asking, "Am I pushing wrong?" Now this may seem like a strange question to ask, but in that moment, I remembered when I had my son. There I was in my mind with a different doctor but the same task at hand. I remembered when that doctor told me to push, but because I had never given birth, I only knew to do what I had seen done on TV, namely, the soap operas. I remember hearing that heavy Jamaican accent say, "You're not going to have a baby pushing like that! You've got to push like you're using the bat'room!" After receiving that correction, I began pushing but in the back of my head prayed, "God PLEASE don't let me have this baby and --------- at the same time!" As the memory closed, and I returned at warp speed back to 2013, I realized immediately that what happened with my son was not what was happening with my daughter. Before I knew it, I heard my doctor say to my husband and mother, "I need you to move back!"

Without hesitation, my mom began asking questions. The doctor looked at them both, then looked at my husband and said, "Do you give us permission to use forceps for this procedure?" My husband, seeing the look in my doctor's eyes nodded his head yes and immediately began to pray while messaging our intercessors to pray as well. I looked over to my left to see a nurse preparing two body bags; it did not take long for me to realize that they were preparing those bags for my daughter and I in case we did not make it. My doctor then looked at me and said, "Don't look over there! Keep your eyes on me! I need you to push with EVERYTHING you got! Do you hear me?" I shook my head yes.

The doctor counted down and yelled, "PUSH!" Now for some, you may be in this place right now. You have been pushing and wondering what difference this push will produce, but just as my doctor could not address the questions being asked in the room, this is not a time for questions but instead, ONLY time to push. I heard her instructions crystal clear and began to push! This moment was so intense that there was no room to cry, scream or complain. As I gave it my all, a nurse rushed over, jumped on my stomach and began to push down on me as if she was giving CPR. As she pushed down, and I pushed as well, my doctor pulled Sarai out with the forceps. All I heard on the other end was silence, but I could see and hear people rushing around to get her over to the appropriate area to clean her off and check on her breathing (I was later told that when they got her out, the umbilical cord was wrapped around her neck three times.) The next words I clearly heard were "STAT!" It has often been shared that giving birth is the closest one can get to death but even in this moment I did not realize how close to death I was. During commotion, someone called my phone, and would you believe it was still sitting in the bed with me? I heard it ring, reached down and despite my condition answered.

Me: Hello.

Them: Pastor B?

Me: Yes.

Them: Is the baby here yet?

Me: Yes.

Them: And you answered the phone?

Me: Yes.

Them: Wait! Are they saying STAT? Are you.…...?

Me: Yes.

Them: Oh my God! Hang up!

Me: Ok.

Click. I opened my eyes and looked down to see what looked like a sea of blood completely taking over the floor. The parts that were not covered in blood were covered with nurses' sneaker prints that had stepped in blood and now began redesigning the floor. It was in that moment that I realized that I was beyond close to death and that if given the opportunity, death would come for me while on the brink of delivering my baby. I watched my doctor work with all of her might to repair all the damage that had been done. I laid there shaking, unable to hold myself together.

Once the staff got my daughter ready to be presented and my doctor recovered me, she stood up with the biggest smile on her face and the biggest baby I had ever seen. She held Sarai up and said, "Congratulations! Here's your daughter!" Now while you may be reading this and waiting for me to tell you how I cried, that story is coming but not yet. I looked at her in disbelief and even for a moment denied that she was mine. There was no way that I could believe that something so massive could come out of me. Soon after, they told me that she did not weigh the seven pounds that I mandated was the maximum I could carry – instead, they told me that she weighed in at nine pounds and five ounces! Normally, the hospital only leaves you in recovery for about an hour before taking you to a room; in my case, they kept me in there for hours. Nurses kept coming by and peeking in the room as if they were expecting a different outcome, only to find me alive and shaky, but well. It was not until I was transferred to my own room and later spoke with my doctor that the reality again hit me like a ton of bricks. As she spoke with me, she advised me that they wanted to "check me" to ensure that the repair work they had done on my lower extremities was sufficient. As they laid me on my side, the worst pain I have ever felt hit me and all I could do was scream. My doctor, alarmed, told the nurse to put me on my back again; when she did, the pain immediately stopped. After she asked me an couple of questions and began to feel around, she discovered that my pubic bone had been completely separated. She advised me that I would have to wear a brace around my hip region for up to eight months, would have difficulty getting up and down the stairs and would need to suspend ministering in dance as well. I was devasted, but grateful, because I could have been in a body bag instead of recovering from separated bones. I laid there, holding my daughter and looking at her calm face. As I took the moment in, I remembered my son, my first blessing and the vast difference between the two, but nevertheless, both blessings were beyond my wildest imagination.

Two days later I was discharged to go home. The doctors did not believe that I was ready, but despite my experience and the trauma my body experienced afterwards, I was ready to go home. Ok, let me be honest, they wanted me to stay another day or two but as I told them, "We have church on Sunday at 3:00pm and I just have to be there!" Upon them saying that my pastor would be ok knowing that I could not be there, I said defiantly, "I AM the pastor!" Even as I type this, I shake my head just as they did – looking at me as a miracle but respecting my determination. During this time in

18

ministry, we were hosting church in our home. Every Sunday we would prepare the room, move couches, chairs and tables to accommodate the growing crowd. We arrived at the house and as I got out of the car I did so with a growing gratitude. We got inside and I chose my new seat, the recliner, as my resting place. They brought the basinet close and put our daughter in it. As the people began to come in, all I could do was smile knowing that they all saw the result but did not know the story of how the blessing came forth.

Praise and worship began to go forth – I closed my eyes and tears began to fall. Before I knew it, I felt as if God had taken me out of my body and back to the hospital. This vision led me to the main hallway. As I began to walk, I found my way to the labor and delivery room I was in. I would have had no idea which one it was had it not been for the angel I saw standing at the door, stationed and monitoring the hall and especially, my room. The door opened and I saw every nurse, my doctor, my family and me as if I were a fly on the wall. In this vision there was no fear or even shock, but simply the glory of God in the room. There was another angel stationed where they weighed and prepared our daughter for us. I looked up and saw another angel who's back was against the ceiling of the room and whose wings covered us like a canopy. I looked over and behind my doctor stood another angel, more massive than them all, holding the doctor's hands and directing her every move. As praise and worship went forth in the room in my house, I began weeping uncontrollably. God entrusted me to deliver what I, along with others, believed that I could not. He entrusted me to deliver a miracle much bigger than myself.

CONTRACTION 2:

First Things First

Before we begin to move into a place of "big talk," we must first be assured that we believe what we are "big talking" about. It is easy to desire more or to push for something big, but if you do not believe, it will most certainly deliver a gut punch you are not ready or prepared for.

Jesus answered him, "I assure you *and* most solemnly say to you, unless a person is born again [reborn from above— spiritually transformed, renewed, sanctified], he cannot [ever] see *and* experience the kingdom of God."

John 3:3

There is an indescribable promise waiting in the wings for us, but it requires a changing of the mind and a decision to pursue purpose. Though these words flow freely on this paper it is not easy. As we reflect on December 31, 2020, until now, no one was expecting what we are currently enduring, a pandemic. We have gone from family gatherings to picking the top twenty instead. We have transcended from simply going to the grocery store for a loaf of bread to fighting over Lysol and other necessities that now give off the feeling of finding water in a drought. If it is one thing we can agree with, it would be that we have now come to the understanding of what urgency really means. In January 2020, we probably thought that we had more time to believe, trust, move, and execute but as we sit in this day, we realize that there is no time like the present and if we are going to pursue anything, we must do so without the former hesitation or procrastination recently displayed.

21

The scripture above tells us that in order for one to see AND experience the kingdom of God there must be a place of receiving the fullness of who God is and a consent to being born again, or in other words, trading in the old for the new of all that He provides. I cannot even imagine how many times God has looked at us and shook His head over our acceptance of less than what He has for us. We quote who He is and what He has done and does but do we genuinely believe? We are now in a dispensation where we simply do not have the time to talk about it, but instead must actively PUSH into the reality of it.

According to the Hebrew calendar we are walking into the year 5781 which means, "Widen your mouth in silence." What on earth does that mean and how does widening my mouth in silence help me? Well, this answer is easy - this next year is about action. For more years than we can count, we have either been the victim of a sweet talker or the ringleader of a broken promise themselves. We have found ourselves saying what we will do, knowing deep inside that what we will TO do may not get done. This place of complacency is dangerous as it leads one to demand that God bless them based on their talk, and not on their movement. We must remember, it takes a movement of some kind to initiate a curse; likewise, there is a requirement of movement to destroy a curse and ignite a blessing as well. So here are two questions:

What has been initiated by you (good or bad), and how do you feel as you shed light on these places?

Use this space to jot down your thoughts. (No worries, whatever is being opened up will be closed up as you proceed.)

_____

_____

_____

_____

The truth of the matter is that while we prepare for the blessing, we do not spend a lot of time considering the enemy and his attempts against us. Many have seen what it is that the enemy has tried and used it as their ticket to quit or give up instead of using it as proof of what is on the other side of the battle. It is here that we must consider some key components.

The thief comes only in order to steal and kill and destroy. I came that they may have *and* enjoy life, and have it in abundance [to the full, till it overflows].

John 10:10

This next sentence may sound crazy to you, but I cannot proceed until I make this next statement clear - the enemy is simply fulfilling his purpose. If you go to Job chapter 1 and two you will find that there are two conversations between God and Satan. In both circumstances, the same question is asked — "What are you doing?" Satan, cocky but technically unemployed says, "Going to and fro in the earth!" In other words, he found himself looking for something to do to accomplish purpose. He was so dedicated to his purpose that he had to go through Job to get a job! Now it's your turn - how determined are you to complete your purpose in the earth and why?

_____

_____

_____

_____

_____

_____

Amid delivering purpose, movement is required. Miracle upon miracle in the Word required movement. While in labor and delivery with my daughter, the onset of the trauma was their discovery that our baby was stuck, so therefore something had to be done to catapult movement for the sake of both of our lives. Whether it was belief (mindset), walking (progression) or another instruction, movement played a huge part in the overall result of those challenging moments. Take a moment to share some of the major moves you have made lately.

_____

_____

_____

_____

_____

_____

The truth remains that though God knows we have the propensity to fall, we are equally equipped to recover.

"Simon, Simon (Peter), listen! Satan has demanded *permission* to sift [all of] you like grain; 32 but I have prayed [especially] for you [Peter], that your faith [and confidence in Me] may not fail; and you, once you have turned back again [to Me], strengthen *and* support your brothers [in the faith]."

Luke 22:31-32

What I do not want to you to think is that this grasping of belief is easy, but instead my prayer is that you understand that if you should so choose to pursue it, you must realize who and what you are contending against. Know this also, that you cannot contain any kind of enemy without an acceptance of who God is and a renewal and sanctification unto Him. As we have read above, you are literally fighting someone who has studied you, even before coming

24

in any level of knowledge of who you are. This is not the time to slack up.

12 For our struggle is not against flesh and blood [contending only with physical opponents], but against the rulers, against the powers, against the world forces of this [present] darkness, against the spiritual *forces* of wickedness in the heavenly (supernatural) *places*. 13 Therefore, put on the complete armor of God, so that you will be able to [successfully] resist *and* stand your ground in the evil day [of danger], and having done everything [that the crisis demands], to stand firm [in your place, fully prepared, immovable, victorious].

Ephesians 6:12-13

CONTRACTION 3:

Two Times Two is....

My family on my mother's side is known for twins, and when you are one who does not want twins, it can leave you wondering if you could be the next in line to deliver more than just the one you have prepared for. Psalm 127:3 says this:

Behold, children are a heritage *and* gift from the LORD, The fruit of the womb a reward. Like arrows in the hand of a warrior, So are the children of one's youth. How blessed [happy and fortunate] is the man whose quiver is filled with them; They will not be ashamed When they speak with their enemies [in gatherings] at the [city] gate.

This does not sound bad at all as long as you are prepared. The reality of preparation brings up the word EXPECTATION. Our belief, as we talked about in chapter 2, demands our movement. When we are not moving in expectation the blessing can catch us by surprise.

I remember when my Lead Armor Bearer said to me, "Pastor I hear the sound of thunderous feet!" Now keep in mind, at the time I was looking around at empty chairs and inwardly wondering if we were in the same place. For years, she continued to repeat the words, "I hear the sound of thunderous feet!" As time progressed, no matter the amount of people that showed up and no matter where we were located, we always prepared for the influx. We always checked to ensure that there was enough seating, parking and sufficient restrooms for anyone that needed to use it. Even with five or ten people, we always prepared for up to thirty people or more. On some days, every chair was filled and on others only a few but nevertheless we had to move in expectation of thunderous feet. What dream or vision is sitting in your spirit right now that seems crazy but like a broken record continues to play on repeat in your mind?

_____

_____

_____

_____

_____

_____

When we see people deliver in multiples, our respect and admiration becomes our response. We watch people make the world news as they deliver five, six or more at a time. We watch the documentaries in curiosity over their ability to raise all of those children and still maintain their sanity. So here it is, some of those that we admire are among those who may have had to endure some kind of alternative pregnancy process such as in-utero insemination. This process involves the implantation into a female and while this process is for the hope of achieving one baby, it has been noted that this procedure has significantly increased the possibility of twins for those who have not been able to produce a positive pregnancy on their own.[2] What am I saying? Some people are behind because they refuse to ask for help! Birthing vision may not be conventional – it may not happen the way it happened for your family line before you, but that does not mean that it is not purposed for you! We by nature are called to produce and multiply; the command was expressed to Adam and Eve in this way:

And God blessed them [granting them certain authority] and said to them, "Be fruitful, multiply, and fill the earth, and subjugate it [putting it under your power]; and rule over (dominate) the fish of the sea, the birds of the air, and every living thing that moves upon the earth."

---

[2] https://www.healthline.com/health/pregnancy/chances-of-having-twins#natural-factors

Some of you reading this are about to find yourself delivering in multiples because that is just how far behind you are. If this is you, fret not, God is with you in this moment. For those who have been patiently waiting, there is double waiting for you. If you are one who has been fighting with all of your might to produce, know that even now God is with you and is preparing you for the full manifestation. I wish that I could tell you that no one will say that you can't or you won't; I cannot tell you that, but I can tell you that before you even stepped foot into this world, God gave you the undeniable ability to produce over and over again.

When you think of contractions where your visions and dreams are concerned, what sticks out to you the most? Have you begun to develop at process of accomplishment and if so, what is it?

_____
_____
_____
_____
_____
_____

CONTRACTION 4:

Clear the Fields! Enlarge Your Tent!

**"Enlarge the site of your tent [to make room for more children];
Stretch out the curtains of your dwellings, do not spare them;
Lengthen your tent ropes
And make your pegs (stakes) firm [in the ground].**

Isaiah 54:2

In case you did not know, this place of birthing requires a relentless determination and refusal to leave barren or empty-handed. This place of expansion requires deep roots and a pit-bull kind of grip! This place of manifestation requires eagle-eye vision that causes you to see beyond what you lost and what others may have said you did not deserve and lean in with your full weight, into the promise that God has for you. The above scripture starts out addressing "the barren woman" with the promise that they will bring forth more than one with an open womb. People may read this with utter confusion as they wonder, "how can a closed womb produce more than one that is open?" In order to understand this, you must understand the promise made. We have heard it one million times or more, but it bears repeating with a full and receiving heart, **God's Word never returns void.** It does not matter who tells you that you cannot produce, God's Word stands and remains to be the final authority.

The Word above says, "make room for MORE children!" This denotes a place of OVERFLOW! Can you imagine launching out once

31

and before you can even catch your breath, God says, "Oh yea by the way, this is yours too?" Can you imagine being able to not only have what He showed you but also what He did not? The following echoes the depth of this idea:

Now to Him who is able to [carry out His purpose and] do superabundantly more than all that we dare ask or think [infinitely beyond our greatest prayers, hopes, or dreams], according to His power that is at work within us,

Ephesians 3:20

Note the keywords, "work within US." In other words, we have a part to play as well, and depending on our personal dedication to the Word spoken, we have the opportunity to receive more or less - it is completely up to us. What are some things that God has promised you that based on where you are seem impossible? What word have you been speaking in an effort to keep that vision or dream alive and producing?

_____

_____

_____

_____

_____

_____

Even as you contemplate your responses, I need you to realize just how pivotal you are! I often say that God has way too much going on and has no time to lie to us. Even when the promise seems huge and unable to be compared, we have to take hold of the fact that the word released is true and shall perform. This Word is not based on what other's believe but instead, what God has spoken.

Just as we must expand our tents, we must be willing to relocate them if necessary. In the age we live in we call it "unfriend" and "block", but what about those that do not disappear out of your life when you hit that button? What about those that you have to see everyday or talk to without incident only to realize that your dream is way too big for them? What do you do when you yourself are having a hard time believing it, but share it in faith hoping that someone will catch it and push you into a place of belief? It is not a foreign concept to pick up our tents and move! We find in the Word, Jesus telling the man at the pool to pick up his bed and walk! Now to some this sounds extremely rude as he had been that way for thirty-eight years, but Jesus had to call the man into a place of decision. What are YOU deciding to do today? What are YOU shifting into as of this very moment?

_____
_____
_____
_____
_____
_____

CONTRACTION 5:

But Wait! My "Parts" Don't Work!

When Abram was ninety-nine years old, the [a]LORD appeared to
him and said, "I am [b]God Almighty;
Walk [habitually] before Me [with integrity, knowing that you
are always in My presence], and be blameless *and* complete [in
obedience to Me].
"I will establish My covenant (everlasting promise) between Me
and you,
And I will multiply you exceedingly [through your
descendants]."

Genesis 17:1-4

Hold up! Wait? What? Did you all see what I saw? Did this
just say, "When Abraham was ninety-nine years old"? Yes, that is
exactly what is says. The Lord gave Abraham a promise of
EXPANSION when he was ninety-nine years old. Can you imagine
living that long with no heir? Keep in mind, we have no doubt that
Abraham asked for one, but it took all this time for God to release
it to him. Now, in previous years it was customary for a couple to get
married young and immediately begin working on having a family.
You know, the 2.5 kids, dog and white picket fence mentality?
Nowadays, it is not foreign to see people wait longer to get married
and potentially even longer before having children. We see people
of high caliber, those in the public light especially, having children at
forty-five and even fifty years old. One of the most iconic figures
ever, Janet Jackson, had a baby at fifty years old! Fifty! Now before
you say, "Well, that's Janet," know this, you too can multiply,

35

regardless of your age, potentially in the natural but most definitely in the spirit. Earlier this year, The New York Post released an article entitled,

"57-year old is one of the oldest women to give birth: 'We've beat the odds!'"

In this article, among the story of this modern-day miracle we find these words,

[3]The oldest mother that was reported <u>by Guinness World Records</u> to deliver a child after conceiving naturally was 59. In 2019, a 74-year-old woman from southern India had twin girls via IVF and is reportedly the oldest woman ever to give birth, <u>according to USA Today</u>.

Now granted, being that this 74-year-old woman became pregnant through the help of medical technology, this was not necessarily a surprise to her husband. Ladies can you imagine being this "seasoned," all of your children have grown and moved on or maybe you do not have children at all, and at the age when you should be enjoying life you now bring home the news of pregnancy? Let's have some fun shall we – Ladies, what would be his response? GO!

_____
_____
_____
_____

_____

[3] 57-year-old is one of the oldest women to give birth (nypost.com)

The truth of the matter is, though it be a spiritual impartation, the difficulty of this news hits there, too. Prophetic Words are spoken with no regard to age and oftentimes, situation. There are people every day receiving Prophetic declarations that they feel ill-equipped to handle. Take for instance, try telling someone sixty, seventy or eighty years old that God is about to give them a DO OVER. Now, if you told a younger person, they would probably run or shout depending on the weight of this news, but oh my, the challenges that could arise for the one receiving this Word in the last stage of their life so to speak. The prophet resounds,

"It's not too late!"

The congregation goes up in an uproar as they push to encourage the receiver of this mighty Word. The praise in the background tries to drown out doubt while the human mind tries to make sense of it all.

"I'm too old."

"There isn't enough time?"

"Will I even live to see this come to pass?"

This, my friend is where we see the promise of God take shape, as he tells Abraham that as he remains committed and fixed on God's will for his life, he will have what has been spoken to him. I have said this before in a previous writing and will say it again now,

In order for a word to manifest, it requires the same posture of the heart that was present when the promise was delivered.

As you continue to read Genesis 17, you find that on the onset of the news, Abraham worships, but then Genesis 17:17 shows up.

¹⁷ Then Abraham fell on his face and laughed, and said in his heart, "Shall a child be born to a man who is a hundred years old? And shall Sarah, who is ninety years old, bear a *child*?"

Now, this is for those who proudly declare that God knows your heart, and as the remaining portion also declares, "and He will reward you according to it." (Jeremiah 17:10). It is at this stage in the conversation that the same news that once made Abraham worship, now causes him to laugh, not out of expectation but out of doubt. Use this space to note some areas that God has promised to you that at this point in your mind seem impossible.

_____
_____
_____
_____
_____
_____

Okay, so let's look at the biological perspective, shall we? Hold on, this conversation is about to become uncensored. I found a question online submitted to a website called www.emedicinehealth.com. In it, a thirty-five-year-old man submitted a question about his inability to "perform." He stated,

[4]"I'm only 35, but the other day I was being intimate with my partner the other day and had trouble maintaining an erection. I'm not ready for impotence this young! I thought ED was a problem just for older guys."

The doctor's response read as follows:

The most common sexual problem in men as they age is erectile dysfunction (ED). In general, the younger a man is, the better his sexual function will be. About 40% of men are affected by erectile dysfunction at age 40, and nearly 70% of men are affected by ED by the time they turn 70.

Now as we bring this into perspective, biology is not a "new" phenomenon, so it likely that Abraham would have experienced this problem as well. For some of us, it feels like God is releasing a promise to use in a time when we believe that our body parts cannot even produce "that" anymore. Could it be that Abraham began to laugh beyond his doubt and in justification of his impotence? I mean, at this point he had his son Ishmael, but no one knows but him and Hagar how difficult it could have been for all of the biological factors to come in alignment long enough for her to walk away from that moment, pregnant. The sad truth is that this move was only made because of then Abram and Sarai's inability to wait on God and the assumption that this was the only way to guarantee him an heir, but I digress. But wait, there is more — this is just The Lord's conversation with Abraham, we have not even gotten to Sarah's response yet.

---

[4] What Is the Average Age for Erectile Dysfunction? (emedicinehealth.com)

Bear in mind, that despite this major moment in time, Abraham has not yet told his wife, but instead remains in a place of process, I guess! Genesis 18 comes, and Abraham is approached by The Lord. When he looks up, he notices three men in his presence. He immediately runs from the tent door and goes to greet them.

3 and Abraham said, "My [a]lord, if now I have found favor in your sight, please do not pass by your servant [without stopping to visit]. 4 Please let a little water be brought [by one of my servants] and [you may] wash your feet, and recline *and* rest comfortably under the tree. 5 And I will bring a piece of bread to refresh *and* sustain [b]you; after that you may go on, since you have come to your servant." And they replied, "Do as you have said."

Abraham runs in the tent and tells Sarah to prepare what he offered their guests. Upon his return they have one question,

"Where is Sarah your wife?"

Abraham advises that she is in the tent. In that moment, the promise of expansion is repeated but this time Sarah hears it.

10 He said, "I will surely return to you at this [e]time next year; and behold, Sarah your wife will have a son." And Sarah was listening at the tent door, which was behind him. 11 Now Abraham and Sarah were old, well advanced in years; she was past [the age of] childbearing. 12 So Sarah laughed to herself [when she heard the LORD'S words], saying, "After I have become old, shall I have pleasure *and* delight, my lord (husband) being also old?" 13 And the LORD asked Abraham, "Why did Sarah laugh [to herself], saying, 'Shall I really give birth [to a child] when I am so old?' 14 Is anything too difficult *or* too wonderful for the [f]LORD? At the appointed time, when the season [for her delivery] comes, I will return to you and Sarah will have a son." 15 Then Sarah denied it, saying, "I

40

**did not laugh"; because she was afraid. And He (the LORD) said,
"No, but you did laugh."**

Like her husband did, Sarah laughs. She laughs! Like us, it is in places like these that we ask as she did, "Lord NOW you want to give me this? I don't even know if I have the strength to enjoy it!" Note here, she has already disqualified her ability to produce, not based off her desire, but on her age and what seems "right to man." How many times has God made a promise to us and we laughed because based on man's timetable it seemed like it could not happen for us? How many times have you desired to have what God said and, in your soul, anticipation was your response, but it was quickly overshadowed by the opinion or expectation of man? Have you ever been there? How did you recover from it? Are you still in it? Take a moment to share.

_____
_____
_____
_____
_____
_____

So then, how do we transition from this laughter of doubt to laughter of assuredness? As we read the scriptures above, we find that Abraham nor Sarah has the chance to stay in this place long. Like I share with every mentee,

"Have your moment, but don't have it long!"

The Word has already been released, and if we do the math that means that they have about ninety days to get over where they are, get on one accord and produce this baby! Yes, you heard it here first people — this baby is not coming forth via a stork or a surrogate, not this time. This time, the promise will be delivered through the vessel it was promised to. This time the promise will be delivered through YOU, laughter and all!

41

[37] For with God nothing [is or ever] shall be impossible."

Luke 1:37

CONTRACTION 6:

Come On In The Room - Or Not!

[a]¹Blessed [fortunate, prosperous, and favored by God] is the man who does not walk in the counsel of the wicked [following their advice and example],
Nor stand in the path of sinners,
Nor sit [down to rest] in the seat of [b]scoffers (ridiculers). ²But his delight is in the law of the LORD,
And on His law [His precepts and teachings] he [habitually] meditates day and night. ³And he will be like a tree *firmly* planted [and fed] by streams of water,
Which yields its fruit in its season;
Its leaf does not wither;
And in whatever he does, he prospers [and comes to maturity].

Psalm 1:1-3

I remember the security setup at the hospital where I delivered my children. Before a person could even gain access, they had to be able to provide a state-issued, picture I.D. for entry. This practice has extended from just applying to the maternity wing, to now, every wing in the hospital. It is almost as if the hospital has now realized the importance of who has the right to gain access through the place of a person's vulnerability.

This wisdom is just as important when it comes to who can be in the room with you during the delivery process. Sometimes, we can be so excited over the mere idea of delivery, that we neglect to be mindful over who gains access to the room. For me, my doctor asked me ahead of time to decide who would be in the room with me and in my opinion, there was no doubt that it would be my Husband and my mother. I knew that neither of these people would freak out at the sight of blood and would push me into my expected end. I knew without a doubt that they would not mistake the blood I had to shed for death, but instead, the beginning of something beautiful. Maybe you are reading this and realizing that you took some baby shower

43

people into the birthing room with you - they were excited when they heard the news and were happy to bring gifts but have no ability to last through the bloody process of bringing the promise forth. Maybe they passed the I.D. process at the security check-in but should have never been on-site for the birth of this promise? Let's talk about it – What are your list of requirements as it relates to who can be in the birthing room? Have you even considered it? Remember, cheers do not mean agreement!

_____

_____

_____

_____

_____

_____

Our focus scripture shares some major nuggets that I want to share with you now. Are you ready? Let's go!

1. **You must find and connect with those who AGREE with your ability to produce God's promise!** (Psa.1:1)

   It is a bad thing not to believe in yourself, but even worse when you connect with those who do not believe in your either. It was a GOD move for Abraham to be approached by the Lord in the form of three men. The Father already knew that had Abraham taken the news to Sarah on his own it could have caused an outward response that would have crushed any expectation that Abraham adopted. Instead, the confirmation came in the form of three men who spoke to it boldly and without question.

2. **You must decide to rest and delight in God's presence and His selection of you! This cannot be a haphazard approach, but a DAILY approach.** (Psa.1:2)

44

To be chosen by God at ANY age is an honor. Jeremiah 1 emphasizes just how "selected" we are by Him. Even when it seems impossible for us to deliver what He has spoken, we must know and trust that He will fulfill His Word if we continue to seek His face and His hand through the process.

3. **Get ROOTED into God's Word concerning your life. Remain strong, immovable and allow His presence to feed the promise He has spoken.** (Psa.1:3)

One of the most fatal movements when can make from a position like this is to uproot ourselves from where the presence of God is. In this verse it says that the tree will be planted by the rivers of water, in other words, planted by Holy Spirit. When we decide that "we" can handle what God has planted, we endanger not only the process but the end results as well.

As you continue to read this amazing testament of Sarah giving birth to Isaac, you will find that she also has the honor of feeding him from her own breast. Yes, not only did God enable her to conceive and give birth, but also gave her the ability to produce milk for the gift that God promised her. Don't you know? Don't you see? God's got you! He is with you! He would never promise you something and leave you alone to figure out the how! God provides for what He promises and through you will manifest just what He has spoken!

Take this moment to write out the promises that will require your full commitment and deeply rooted dedication to produce in this season. No worries, you've got this!

_____
_____
_____
_____
_____
_____

And if you need more space, go for it! This space is yours!

CONTRACTION 7:

Suspended Labor

⁶I am convinced *and* confident of this very thing, that He who has begun a good work in you will [continue to] perfect *and* complete it until the day of Christ Jesus [the time of His return].

Philippians 1:6

During labor and delivery, the woman experiences this massively uncomfortable place, the contraction which we discussed in chapter four. Many of people have had baby showers where they apply a device to a man just to allow him to feel what contractions feel like in the natural. When it first starts, they look rather unbothered, but as often is the case, the more that intensity applied, the more they realize how grateful they are to be a man.

I remember giving birth to my children. I do not have the testimony of my water breaking at home, but instead had to be induced both times. By definition, induce means,

**(1) succeed in persuading or influencing (someone) to do something.
(2) bring about or give rise to.**

Based on the experience with my son, and the length of time that I was pregnant with my daughter, I concluded that it must have been mighty comfortable in there, because neither were making a move to move out! I want you to think for a moment,

What vision or dream have you been holding onto way too long?

_____

_____

_____

_____

_____

_____

You see, as I shared before, the longer my babies stayed in my belly, the more uncomfortable I got, but here is the catch, they were not uncomfortable enough to break out! Yes, you heard me right, BREAK OUT! The conditions seemed perfect, and the temperature was just right, but there was a purpose waiting for them to embark upon that required them to break out first. As science has taught us, when a baby stays in well beyond their time, the fluids and current environment can turn on them, and ultimately cause their untimely death. What my babies did not know was that if they refused to come out, they would HAVE to be induced as a method of saving their life. They were complacent but had they stayed in too long, that same place of comfort would have become a perfect storm for their demise.

Now let's tackle this since we are here - you may be reading this right now and realize that maybe you haven't birthed the dream because you love the benefits of pregnancy. SAY WHAT? You heard me right! Maybe you are holding onto the dream because it gets you a certain level of attention, good parking spaces and makes room for great conversation. Maybe you keep holding on because you love the idea of producing but are not ready for the reality of how life will change once you give birth? Can you imagine me showing up at the hospital, being induced, getting my epidural and telling the doctor NO when it is time to get ready to push? Can you imagine someone, with their legs in the stirrup and everything, only to take a

48

breath and say, "You know, this was more than bargained for. I'm going to go home, think this over and come back when it makes more sense." Not only would everyone in the room look at them like they were crazy, but they would also advise her that leaving at that point would be too dangerous and detrimental and basically, refuse her ability to leave for the sake of her life and the life of the baby she is carrying. Some of you are reading this right now and realizing that you decided to get off the table when it was time to push. Everything around you became more important.

Everyone else's goals and dreams superseded yours, so you put it on hold, and quite honestly, it is still "on hold."

You looked around at your family line and realizing that no one else had accomplished such a task, and decided that it wasn't for you either, even though you have carried it to term.

Wanting this "baby" is not the question but being properly prepared for it is. Sometimes this thought makes us believe that to give it away would be better than finding our hidden superpower.

Even in your tsunami of doubt you must remember this: God chose you because He knew that you could handle it. When He knew that no one else had done it, He chose you. When He knew that there would be times that you would look to the heavens and simply but powerfully say, "God what in the world!", He still chose you. Even as I type these words, this song comes to mind. It was once one that would cause tears to fall every time I sang it, and today, even the more.

[5]He loves me even when I fall beneath His will
He loves me, oh, oh, oh, He loves me
When my broken heart just won't keeps still
He loves me oh, oh, oh, He loves me
Even though He knew sometimes I'd fall
Yet and still my name He called, He loves me
Jesus, I'm so grateful for Your love
He loves me even though I was born in sin
He loves me, oh, oh, oh, He loves me, yeah
Took me like I was and now I'm free again, yeah
He loves me, yeah, oh, oh, oh, He loves me

Let's do the hard thing. Let's consider some things that you did not think you had the ability to birth, but you really do. Ready? Go!

_____

_____

_____

_____

_____

_____

---

[5] "He Loves Me" / Kirk Franklin and the Family, 1998

CONTRACTION 8:

Post-Partum

[27] For this child I prayed, and the LORD has granted me my request which I asked of Him.

1 Samuel 1:27

You may be reading this right now and saying what I have said one million times or more,

"But I didn't even WANT this!"

During the process of conception and now, delivery, you have grown to love this beautiful miracle. Your body is producing all your miracle needs for its growth, and yet there remains a void. This should be the greatest moments of one's life, but for some it brings a reaction of sadness, detachment, anger, resentment and yes, inadequacy.

Postpartum is documented to consist of three separate areas – postpartum, postpartum depression and postpartum psychosis.

Postpartum ("baby blues") - [6]commonly include mood swings, crying spells, anxiety and difficulty sleeping. Baby blues typically begin within the first two to three days after delivery and may last for up to two weeks. Symptoms include: mood swings, anxiety, sadness, irritability, feeling overwhelmed, crying, reduced concentration, appetite problems and trouble sleeping.

---

[6] Postpartum depression - Symptoms and causes - Mayo Clinic

Postpartum Depression - may be mistaken for baby blues at first — but the signs and symptoms are more intense and last longer and may eventually interfere with your ability to care for your baby and handle other daily tasks. Symptoms usually develop within the first few weeks after giving birth, but may begin earlier, during pregnancy, or later, up to a year after birth. Depressed mood or severe mood swings. Symptoms include: excessive crying, difficulty bonding with your baby, withdrawing from family and friends, loss of appetite or eating much more than usual, inability to sleep (insomnia) or sleeping too much, overwhelming fatigue or loss of energy, reduced interest and pleasure in activities you used to enjoy, intense irritability and anger, fear that you're not a good mother, hopelessness, feelings of worthlessness, shame, guilt or inadequacy, diminished ability to think clearly, concentrate or make decisions, restlessness, severe anxiety and panic attacks, thoughts of harming yourself or your baby and recurrent thoughts of death or suicide.

Without help, postpartum depression can morph into something called Postpartum Psychosis.

Postpartum Psychosis - a rare condition that typically develops within the first week after delivery — the signs and symptoms are severe. Signs and symptoms may include: confusion and disorientation, obsessive thoughts about your baby, hallucinations and delusions, sleep disturbances, excessive energy and agitation, paranoia and attempts to harm yourself or your baby.

Now this seems like a heavy price to pay for something you never even asked for, nevertheless, maybe you have experienced these very emotions not just in the physical but in the spiritual, too. When one launches out into a great vision, in their head they see all the people there, every item selling out and chairs filled from wall to wall only to find the room empty and waiting. If we are not careful and dedicated to the cause, we can allow this place to lead us into a place of depression and doubt and this feeling does not care about who you are or what your title is. In a previous release of mine, Rehobeth Church Road: Suicide in the Pulpit, I shared how I processed

52

through the attempt to take my own life in January 2017. That Sunday was unimaginable, and after what was seen as a successful time of impartation in a fleeting moment it all seemed to come crashing down around me. Within hours, I went from worship to warfare, as the thoughts filled my head from the enemy of how the current condition of our church was my fault, but if I committed suicide, it would make everything okay. In that moment, inadequacy filled my mind, and it did not matter how many people's lives were touched by God using me, simply put, I just wanted to die. Here we were, birthing purpose in our church and in the community and I found myself facing the lie that though I had birthed something great, there was nothing in me that had the ability to sustain it. I do not know who this is for, and had no intention of even going this way, but in this moment, God needs you to be real with you.

What are you afraid of? Where is the inadequacy? Is it something that someone spoke over you? Is it the fear of, "what if it WORKS?" What is it?

_____
_____
_____
_____
_____
_____
_____
_____
_____
_____
_____
_____
_____

Now, in this same moment I want you to stop, breathe and listen. God chose YOU for this blessing. You, my dear are able to handle every challenge that arises with this place. Depression is not your portion and anxiety is not either. You have been chosen to accomplish this great purpose and out of all the people in the world, He gave it to YOU. In you there is a strength to complete! In you there is a determination to finish! In you there is a victory awaiting. In you, there is His purpose to fulfill.

You've got this, you've got THIS.

Take this moment, take this space, to write a note to the future you! Declare! Decree! (Now, keep in mind, this person has been waiting for a long time to come out, and you have the key.)

_____
_____
_____
_____
_____
_____
_____
_____
_____
_____
_____
_____
_____
_____
_____
_____
_____
_____
_____
_____
_____
_____
_____
_____
_____
_____
_____

CONTRACTION 9:

Destiny Arising

⁶ I am convinced *and* confident of this very thing, that He who has begun a good work in you will [continue to] perfect *and* complete it until the day of Christ Jesus [the time of His return].

Philippians 1:6

When Steven Maraboli was asked about his thoughts concerning destiny, he said this:

"Letting go means to come to the realization that some people are a part of your history, but not a part of your destiny."

All of us can attest to the fact that when one brings a new life into the world, LIFE CHANGES. This is one of those major changes where we realize who is dependable and who can handle the new US that has emerged. It is in this book and the fragments of these chapters that we have all had to take at least one selah moment to truly consider who can handle our place of destiny. It is in this realm that we must take that pause and that breath to realize that everyone that got the birth announcement may not be able to handle the depth of what this blessing requires, and if that be the case, it is still okay.

There is Word going around in this season that is being echoed from the generations of the earth called "elevation". As we have watched the pandemic sweep through and remove what the church world refers to as "Generals," we are also faced with the reality of who will carry the mantle next and who the next successor will be. Even if we have not had the audacity to ask this in public, we have indeed asked this in private and found ourselves seeking clarity for what life without that kingdom voice will look like. The truth of the matter is, that even in this place of immense pain, destiny is indeed arising in this world. The need for voices who are not afraid and for those who will truly cry loud and spare not is crying from the ground. The graveyards of dreams and visions never realized are crying from their cemetery plots realizing that they have been buried with the one who had the ability to birth them into the world but never believed big enough to do so.

The sad reality we face is that most kingdom voices are not sought after until it is too late. Generals whose voices were not even in demand on social media or YouTube alike, are found to be trending after their voice is gone. This is not just true in the "gospel arena" but in this world. The movie we have since overlooked or gotten over becomes a sold-out DVD at the sound of the main character's demise. In other words, we realize when destiny has greeted us but oftentimes lack the appreciation of it until it is too late. Can you imagine how loud the voice of your destiny is? Maybe you have heard it speak in the middle of the night or found yourself having daydreams about it. Have you honestly considered the strength of your sound and what your destiny is calling for in this hour? Ezekiel 37 says it like this:

3 And He said to me, "Son of man, can these bones live?" And I answered, "O Lord GOD, You know."

Oh baby! Now this can turn out to be something! If you read the preceding verses, you will find out that before The Lord did anything else, he took Ezekiel out in the spirit. Destiny is calling but sometimes its call can be overwhelming, why, because maybe just maybe we are trying to greet it in our own strength and power. Note this, it was the HUMAN side of Jesus that said, "take this cup from me," but it was the spirit of God in Him that said,

"Not my will by thine be done!" (Luke 22:42 KJV)

How about this — it is not that you cannot do it or cannot have it, you just have to step out of yourself to see that it is FOR YOU! Now let's go a step further - what happens when you have spoken the worst for so long that destiny agrees? If we read further into Ezekiel 37, we find this:

¹¹ Then He said to me, "Son of man, these bones are the whole house of Israel. Behold, they say, 'Our bones are dried up and our hope is lost. We are completely cut off.'

In other words, what happens when the words of disbelief obey and take root? Well, there must be a YOU that emerges so relentlessly that it causes every doubt spoken, even your own to be silenced. Bear this in mind, the entire time that this now "exceeding great army" was speaking, they were still standing in their same place, in the grave where they were left. Reading this chapter not only do we find that by God's Word the army comes back to its rightful place, but even the more we find that tendons, joints, and everything is restored, even down to their breath.

So, you may say,

"I've said so much! How will I ever overcome this?!"

Well, the truth is simple yet powerful, SPEAK SOMETHING ELSE! Listen, you have spoken the worst of it, and you are seeing the manifestation of it. Like my Husband once said, "There is nothing wrong with your reach!" Now, you just have to learn how to REACH RIGHT! We began this process in the previous chapter - DECREE! DECLARE! The same strength you used to believe that it could not work is the same strength and more that you must now apply to reverse it! The same attitude you had about demise, must now turn into determination that you will never have to see that place again. Just as The Lord changed Abram to Abraham and Sarai to Sarah, there is a name change in store for you as well. Destiny has been waiting for you to get here! Destiny has been waiting for you to produce here, and this time not in struggle, but in boldness and power! Destiny has been waiting for you to arise out of your low place and accept the beauty of manifestation that it is waiting on you.

Be not afraid of the conception.

Be not afraid of the pregnancy.

Be not afraid of the labor.

Be not afraid of the delivery.

Be not afraid of the breathing.

Be not afraid of the push.

It is all necessary for the greatness that is waiting on you!

Now declare your pursuit! This time shout it out, embrace it, mean it, OWN IT. It is waiting on YOU.

It's time.

_____

_____

_____

_____

_____

_____

_____

_____

_____

_____

_____

_____

_____

_____

_____

_____

_____

_____

_____

_____

_____

_____

_____

_____

_____

_____

Brandi L. Rojas

Wife I Mother I Pastor I Author I Mentor I Entrepreneur I Visionary

Pastor Brandi L. Rojas is a native and resident of Greensboro, N.C. She serves with her Husband, Pastor Omar Rojas at Maximizing Life Family Worship Center in Greensboro, N.C., a vision God birthed through them in 2015. Rojas has been in Dance Ministry for over 20 years and is a 2009 graduate of the School of Disciples taught under the late Bishop Otis Lockett, Sr. Pastor Rojas was licensed to preach the Gospel on February 27, 2011, in Thomasville, N.C., and as a result DYmondFYre Global Ministries was born. Rojas was ordained as an Ordained Elder June 2012, was installed as Pastor with her Husband, Pastor Omar Rojas in January 2013 and now serves as Executive Pastor for the vision God has assigned to them through #MaxLife.

Since that time, she and her Husband, also known as #TeamRojas, by God's mandate, have been honored in the marketplace and birthed several evangelistic causes. In 2013, Rojas was named Sweetheart of the Triad, an award given based on community involvement. In January 2014, Rojas opened FYreDance Studios and Liturgical Arts Consulting which provides on-site instruction, virtual teaching, consultation services, choreography services and deliverance and healing dance encounters. In that same year, after serving with Pastor Cassandra Elliott and The Gathering Experience for two years, she began serving and currently serves as the Lead Dance Vessel Coordinator for this time of worship amongst those who are hungry, thirsty and desperate for the presence of God. The following year a prayer walk initiative was created to bring the local churches and community together to work together and help lead the lost to Jesus Christ and empower the world through a vehicle called The Gatekeeper's Legacy; she has also served as part of the planning and leadership committee for the National Day of Prayer for the City of Greensboro and currently serves as the youngest committee member, only African American and only female on the core team.

In February 2016, Rojas launched out again through the mandate of women's ministry. IgniteHerSoul International Women's Fellowship (formally The Legacy Ladies Fellowship.) This serves as an organization created to help women of God pray, push and live the reality of what God has called them to do. Most recently to this list of mandates, The CrossOver Resource Center was added, working to provide solutions for life's transitions to the community. Rojas released her first book in June 2016 entitled In the Face of Expected Failure and her sophomore project, Humpty Dumpty in Stilettos: The

Great Exchange, in November 2016. It was with the second book release Fiery Beacon Publishing House was launched, serving current and upcoming authors, playwrights, poets, blog writers and more. Humpty Dumpty in Stilettos was nominated for the national Literary Trailblazer of the Year Award in June 2017 by the Indie Author Legacy Award in Baltimore, Maryland and in July 2017 she was noted as an International Best-Selling Author for her part in a collaborative effort called Stories from the Pink Pulpit: Women in Ministry Speak. Rojas is also a two-time nominee for Trailblazer of the Year, Choreographer of the Year and Women of Inspiration with ACHI Women Supporting Women, Inc. She is currently preparing for her next solo release, Rehobeth Church Road: Suicide in the Pulpit and is celebrating the first publishing company collaboration for Fiery Beacon Publishing House entitled, When Legacy Arises from the Threshing Floor: A Collective of Trials and Tribulations Superseded by Undeniable Triumphs!

In the Marketplace, Pastor Rojas is also known for her progressive efforts through her travel company, DYmondFYre Destinations and the international platform of Surge365 where she makes it a priority to share the reality and necessity of multiple streams of income which empowers the home, community, nation and world. Pastor Rojas is grateful and humbled at how God continues to expand the entire vision, not just to the United States, but internationally as well. #Team Rojas are the proud parents of five children. Pastor Brandi Rojas is a Worshiper, Servant, Praise Vessel, and Prayer Warrior, but most of all, she is a vessel who is on fire for God.

Wife I Mother I Pastor I Author I Mentor I Entrepreneur I Visionary

Maximizing Life Family Worship Center

https://www.facebook.com/MaximizingLife/

Phone: (336) 497-1897

Fiery Beacon Publishing House

(Consulting/Publishing Group)

https://www.facebook.com/FieryBeaconCPG/

Fiery Beacon Travel

https://www.facebook.com/thelegacybuilder/

IgniteHerSoul International Women's Fellowship

https://www.facebook.com/ignitehersouliwf/

Phone: (501) 500-3973 (FYRE)

IG and Twitter: @allthingsdymondfyre and @maxlifefwc

Fiery Beacon
PUBLISHING HOUSE

Greensboro, North Carolina

Phone: (336) 285-5794

fierybeaconcpg@gmail.com

Become a part of our #FYreLitNation family by visiting:

https://www.linktr.ee/fierybeaconpublishinghousellc

Get your other Fiery Beacon favorites by

Pastor Brandi Rojas today!

In the Face of Expected Failure

Humpty Dumpty in Stilettos: The Great Exchange

When Legacy Arises from the Threshing Floor:
Trials and Tribulations Superseded by Undeniable Victories

Stories from the Pink Pulpit: Women in Ministry Speak
(Collaboration by Dr. Marilyn E. Porter)

My Pink Stilettos
(Collaboration by Apostle Larita Rice-Barnes)

Rehobeth Church Road: Suicide in the Pulpit

Before You Hit 40: 41 Povitol Wisdom Nuggets

Build It A-GAIN: Confessions of the Nehemiah Generation

(Fall 2021)

Talitha Koum: Get Up Little Girl, Get Up! (Fall 2021)

69

www.ingramcontent.com/pod-product-compliance
Lightning Source LLC
LaVergne TN
LVHW051710080426
835511LV00017B/2832